waterways series

The Kitchen of Lovely Contraptions

releasing new voices, revealing new perspectives

The Kitchen of Lovely Contraptions

waterways series
www.waterways-publishing.com
an imprint of flipped eye publishing

Acknowledgments are due to the following publications in which some of these poems first appeared: The London Magazine, Magma Poetry, Fuselit, Equinox, Trespass, Acumen, Envoi, Equinox, and the anthologies Shape Sifting and Images of Women.

Triumph Triple R and *The Lives of Neighbours* were both placed in the Ware Poetry Competition, *Lost Property* was commended in the Ver Poets Competition and *Lambskin* won first prize in the Ledbury Poetry Competition.

ISBN-13: 978-1-905233-32-8

Editorial work for this book was supported by the Arts Council of England.

The text is typeset in Palatino from Linotype GmbH.

LOTTERY FUNDED

for Robin

The Kitchen of Lovely Contraptions

Jacqueline Saphra
2011

Acknowledgements

I owe a debt of gratitude to all the people who have helped this collection on its way through a combination of support and tough love especially Norbert Hirschhorn, Penelope Shuttle, Polly Clark, Mimi Khalvati and the APW. Thanks also to Roddy Lumsden for the commissions, to my friends and colleagues at The Vineyard, to my editor, Jacob Sam-La Rose and to Nii Parkes at flipped eye.

Big love to Imogen Barford, Bridget de Courcy, Alexandra Abraham and Kate Lock for all the cappuccinos and encouragement, to Uncle Robbie for teaching me about persistence, to my tolerant and inspirational children, and most of all to Robin for keeping the faith.

Contents

III

When I was a child I tied my mother and father together with bandages and put a song in their mouths. If I wound them up they sang an Afrikaans duet in perfect thirds. Our house was filled with cookers, stethoscopes, fridges, small hammers and secretaries taking dictation. I sat quietly on an ink blotter while mother plaited my hair and father listened to my heart.

I

Jankel

I never knew you Jack, or was it Jankel,
but they named me after you. I heard you stank
of shtetl Jack, your accent made them call you
jew. You never ditched your Litvak twang,
my mother said. Your brothers with the knack
for shekls took you to the bank, bought you a desk,
a white coat and a stethoscope, made you Dr. Jack.
Oh Grandpa Jack, you crazy Stalinist, caught
on camera with the red flag, Edinburgh, May Day
nineteen-thirty-two, you leftist hack, the man
whose eyes were sad and black, who knows
what you'd been through? You left me clues:
this, your scratched consulting desk, a streak
of melancholy, tracks of dust and sepia, your name.
These words are all that I can give you back.

An Unofficial History

It must have been at night and no doubt they kept
the light on because each of them liked to watch
whatever they were touching and desired moreover
to be seen. And what a night it was, of steam and invocation,
mutters, cries and wishes, miraculous lust, irrevocable

human error. Sometimes the most unlikely combinations
can produce a tangible result. Strange to think that just
the common heave and thrust, the usual universal ecstasy
could be their marriage glue, transcend, over years, such rank
incompatibility. As unofficial chronicler of that night, I believe

there must have been a mutual outrageous climax, that
it was a pivotal experience imbued with unexpected
gravitas, as was the bracing follow-up, that twitching race
of the ridiculous, those nearly-beings making for one huge
stranded cell ripe for the breaching, programmed

for a kind of mad union, that two half-lives might be salvaged
to make a whole. I can't say I was there precisely but I swear
my floating soul was witness to this chance, the sweetest, gravest
and most typical of mistakes and that this story was laid down
in my bones, because I was waiting, willing to be conjured.

Visiting My Father, 1964

A vertical ascent, *so wrong without a man,*
rattle of hat-racks.

My mother held the blandest of boiled smiles
though her face was green.

She wore her tremor like an old blanket,
shaming, familiar.

She took their miniatures, allowed their songs
of rocks or no rocks

as cold rolls came with long life milk,
rare rush of Coca-Cola.

My mother slept. Safe hours slipped
the surface of wings,

the plane spun clouds and blue,
the sun made spots.

I fashioned a man of toothpicks
and chocolate.

Descent was turbulent; mother woke to find
the tremor returned. Intimacy

of father fell apart. Landing was hard.
The safety belt unclicked.

Blueprint

I can't remember why I'm here; too pissed
perhaps, or just too naked. The end
is always shame, however hard I twist
away. Love won't budge; a blueprint pinned
inside the crimsoned eye: me, on the sand
before the smiling man again, my breasts
hangdog and sorry, nipples to the wind
and shrunk to tight pink peas. He's dressed
of course, so cool and winning as he bends
towards me with the promise of a kiss.
I thought I'd turned my back on all of this,
but no. The dirty sand still pocks my thighs,
the sea groans in and out. Somebody cries,
the blueprint leaks a stain behind my eyes.

We Come in Peace for all Mankind

I hid behind the sofa.
I wanted this to be a lie
like babies under cabbage leaves
or perhaps some grown-up joke
like Till Death Us Do Part.
I wanted to believe the moon hung
like a helium balloon from the ceiling
of the sky, that it slowly inflated,
then leaked towards the stars.
When the spaceman took one giant leap
into that flat world of black and white,
my mother was in the darkened kitchen
trembling over a carton of Silk Cut
which she was meant to have given up.
My stepfather did not call for her
as the flag stabbed the planet's crust.
I closed my eyes and conjured smarties
raining from a technicolour sky,
friends with antennae, telepathy and silver skin
who understood my language
and spoke it with a broad accent of moon.
I opened the door of my spaceship
and stepped out in my new midi dress
with the purple velvet bow.
They sang me songs a bit like The Kinks
but higher and all along the sea
of tranquillity, they made two columns
for me to walk between.

Look, No Lines

Katie was gone all summer, off with Danish relatives to a place
where everyone was naked all the time even in the cinema

or launderette. The day she came home I was at the door
carrying my usual kit: pink pyjamas, favourite doll, and bag

of pick'n'mix, but Katie had acquired a tan, a mini skirt,
a turntable in a grey box. She flipped the silver catch,

lifted the lid, demonstrated the cleaning brush, speed settings,
diamond stylus. She had a new LP, the one with *that photo*

on the front: a man's crotch, a real fly you could open and close
if you wanted. She showed me how to unsheath the shiny vinyl,

lower the record onto its bed and set it spinning. Hiss and crackle,
then the sound I'd only ever heard from older brothers' rooms

or through the window of some squat down Haverstock Hill:
deafening, electric, immense. Katie took off her T shirt, unzipped

and lowered the mini skirt in one slick move, stepped out
of her knickers. *Look, no lines.* Her body was still smooth

and flat as the doll I pushed down to the bottom of my bag,
but when Katie danced I knew something was over.

I met her Mum in Sainsbury's a few years later and she told me
Katie was working in a strip club in LA. Suddenly behind my eyes

an unexpected slide show: grey box, silver catch, man's crotch
with real zip, white knickers on a parquet floor, a girl who danced.

Pounds Shillings and Pence

Nothing added up
but I could copy
Debbie's columns while
I mused on Mrs Moxon
with a black eye
serving lumpy tapioca
our lodger's visits
to The Clinic
what Groupies were
or Dutch Caps and why
Mr Capener could never
never be my Dad
even though he was
The Hippest Teacher
Debbie told me
with his velvet loons
and sideburns.
He smiled at Debbie
as she showed me
how to carry twelves
and I was lost.
Sums couldn't make
my mother's hands
stop shaking or pay
for a Trinitron
colour TV
just like Debbie's
or explain why
I was nothing
to Mr Capener
just a girl
whose maths book
was a mess.

Target Practice

The adults think it's good for me watch the news.
I'm good at watching. From the window of your room,
on the safe side of the glass, I see the garden world
in colour, not TV monochrome. Today, I plan
to ask them, finally, how close we are to Vietnam.

Next door, Mrs Perkins cheats her pink blooms blue,
with a secret stash of aluminium sulphate.
Mr Perkins rides his deckchair, barley-watered,
counting overs on the radio, while he augments his tan.
I dream of children listening for planes in Vietnam.

Mrs Grigson on the other side is making bread,
the scent of yeast at war with honeysuckle.
Mr Takahashi two doors down tinkers with
his Hovermo and tends his narrow strip of land.
I've heard that children work the paddy fields of Vietnam.

At the far end of the garden, the dented apple tree
shivers in fresh green, expectant, beyond blossom.
Summer floats beyond this window like a baited hook.
I won't go out to play, for fear of Uncle Sam,
not knowing if it's rude to ask how far we are from Vietnam.

Sergeant Pepper's on the spin in your psychedelic room,
your strung-up Airfix warplanes search for targets.
News is vague from Mr Perkins' radio. You arrange a box
against the apple tree, cue up the Coca-Cola cans.
The children stand in line for rice in Vietnam.

You call it *plinking*. I think of amateur guitar.
No danger, you say, just practice. Only an airgun.
Still, I won't come out. I'll stay here, behind the glass,
thinking of napalm, covering my ears with both hands.
I wonder if the children feel like this in Vietnam.

A bullet glances off a can and hits the apple tree again.
I've seen the naked children run in sunny Vietnam.

The Art of Diplomacy

At three I learned to listen, not to chat.
At eight I counselled friends and sorted spats.
By twelve I was a bloody diplomat.

At forty I began to smell a rat
at last. I said to hell with that.
Hand me that baseball bat.

Hot Chip Machine

The slip of a shilling
through the narrow slot
as if into a secret well
of boiling oil.
The salivating wait.

The magic drop
of a polystyrene cup,
vessel for the feast.
Suck of fingers,
sting of salted tongues,

the downhill walk
in short skirts
to the taunts of boys
our mouths raw
with flirt and burn.

Our Mothers knew nothing
of this new diversion.
That cool facade,
the bubbling slick inside,
the risk of fire.

Tattoo

A man with dye and dodgy needles waits
behind the blackened window by the bridge.
Check out his flash: a gaudy bird, a heart,
a manacle, two fuck-you fingers etched
in red. Choose. Then let him excavate
your skin. At first the burn, later the itch.
Irrevocable ink. You may regret
his handiwork; be careful what you wish.
No scalpel cure, no wash-away design;
years later, bend the track-way of your spine,
find yin and yang above the knicker line.
Laser away; old patterns will persist.
Your skin remembers. Try this: clench a fist
or flex an arm and watch the serpent twist.

What I've come to tell you

You really want to know, my heart? Then listen.
This is how I've lived: I once stepped backwards
off a wall for the hell of it, climbed a mountain
in a blizzard with no rope, took my chances
in the bullring - you'll remember I was ungored,
but thrown; I made it happen. Madame Butterfly
tore my heart out at the Met not once, but
three times because I asked for it. You love me
for my gung-ho, my close calls,
                                    so now I'll tell you
why I'm here: some calamities go unremarked
for years. We don't invite them but they visit us.
The dark places of the body often hide a secret
multiplication: a mass has been detected here,
in here, where you can't see it. They'll take
some bits of me for tests. Remember when
I led you blindfold up the street just for fun?
No, I can't do that now, it's late. I'll keep you posted.
Look at the time. Let me go. Where's my coat?
I said, Let me go.

The Lives of Neighbours

I have never been intimate with them, even when their frogs
invaded my garden or their dog ate my fence. I know only

that they sometimes argue but I can't hear what about,
make love silently if at all, often cook with garlic,

frequently receive packages. Just today my doorbell
rang three times. The postman knows my habits.

Each delivery a larger parcel, each an interruption.
It was time to take a look. Inside, I found their lives:

an orchestra that played songs from Oklahoma,
two seats for an obscure Hungarian play, a tupperware

filled with frogspawn. I found his nervous breakdown,
her facelift, two mortarboards, a broken love-seat.

I've wrapped the parcels up again. Nobody will know.
Soon the neighbours will come knocking and I'll smile,

hand over what's theirs, not mentioning all I've stashed away:
one box of milk teeth, a grand piano, their forgotten moon.

Guitar Hero

It's time to dump my body, its mess
of love and organs, deny the chaos

of invention, enter my gyrating avatar,
her edges sharp and famous as I retreat

inside her skin, to dance along this track
of obstacles, beacons that crave reflex,

bypass of unwieldy song: mechanics,
animation, hit after hit to touch

on love in the virtual dark then move on
without regrets or groupies, crack or rider.

I'll pluck those cyber strings, no catgut,
blood or accident, find the perfect beat

of electronic drums in someone else's song
and let my heart be fooled, my flesh be numb.

The Striking Hour

I'm the girl in black with gravitas who rocks
with the pendulum, the one who won't forgive,
the diva who lives and re-lives the drama

of the tick and toll, bruised in the places
where I trip and trip again, running for trains.
Maybe that's why I break so many watches:

I overwork the cogs of memory, wind and rewind,
tune in, tune out of eras till the springs give way.
Though it makes me sick, I travel backwards

too often, stopping at those pinch-points:
what if, if only, where nothing can change.
But sometimes, I see myself humming

on some bright platform, beside a pyramid
of broken clocks. I synchronise my selves,
call them to heel all dressed in lipstick, feathers

of unnatural pink, outrageous tights. I smash
a few plates, kiss somebody, anybody, slur
my sorries into the mic. Make up for lost time.

II

'*Take this waltz, take this waltz,*
take its broken waist in your hands'
                    Leonard Cohen

The Kitchen of Lovely Contraptions

There was once a man who claimed he'd been assaulted
by a woman's underwear. Invited back for coffee,
he'd walked into the kitchen where ranks of brassieres
and panties hung from a ceiling trap in readiness
for ambush. Stockings brushed his cheeks, hooks
and buttons snagged on his hair, straps and ribbons
tied him to a place he'd longed for always without knowing.
As a fine layer of lace wrapped itself around his eyes,
he was breathless, helpless at the pink coal-face
of femininity, and fell into a beautiful swoon.

When he woke, he was captive. His life became
a sweet, slow undoing and re-doing of those fastenings
and – or so the story goes – the coffee never came.

Bodies of Water

Because you make me sway
before we've even touched

the bottle, I have no appetite
for this sea bass, prostrate

on its bed of kombu, no desire
to pop these pearls of caviar

on my tongue, no urge to bend
the spines of flushed crustaceans

dressed and laid on ice,
and I can barely swallow

for the pitch and roll inside, yes
I'm dry and taut as whispers

so come on, loosen me
with daquiris, your mouth

against my ear and tell me again
that you and I are composed

of the same elements, that
there's a sea inside me,

and you, too, are salt and water.
I'll dream up the rest.

The Pick-up

This is the girl
the front seat tramp
with the haversack
and the long cigarette
and the Spanish guitar
and the bong that she smoked
at your side in the car
who spread her legs
on the burning bed
and gave you her heat.

This is the girl
with the sky tattooed
on the soles of her feet
who sat in your truck
full of sugar and salt
the hard-boned bitch
who flicked your switch
at the edge of a cliff
the girl who felt
the bite of your belt
who cut herself free
with a silver knife
and jumped from the bridge.

This is the girl,
with brine for eyes
with floating limbs
and a voice unhinged
who festers and sighs
who gurgles and sings
who laughs at your lies
in her bloated disguise:
your trouble and strife
with the golden ring,
whose scent still clings
to the skin of your life.

Penelope

(*After Cavafy's Ithaka*)

One last act: the loom.
Hurl it against the wall.
Let it splinter. Laugh. Hurry past
your dreaming child and head towards
the water. Chart the stars.

Choose your vessel. Smile to think
that soon your suitors will amble down,
squinting at the sunrise,
check their boats and find one gone
along with you, the prize.

As you hoist the sail, recall
those circles that you've walked
imprisoned on your island home,
waiting for the wayward husband
who might never come.

As you set out from Ithaka,
don't picture the child asleep,
think only of the man you seek.
Keep him always in your mind.
Don't start getting girly-weak.

Have faith. Forget his stories
and the way he's apt to wander,
drink and womanise.
Remember how he felt
between your thighs.

[31]

As Ithaka becomes a distant speck,
as you and your boat are thrown
from crest to trough, hold fast
and look to the horizon;
how good to be alone at last.

At each sunlit harbour bind your breasts.
Weigh anchor, swagger
to the trading post.
Gather treasure: pearl and coral,
ebony, amber, precious stones.

Don't allow your thoughts to wander
to the boy, his soft awakenings
and you not there.
Isn't this for him? Around your neck
carry a small lock of his hair.

When becalmed, don't stay too long.
Haul out your oars and row.
Let your lungs expand,
enjoy the way your muscles grow,
take pleasure in your callused hands.

One afternoon, you catch yourself,
perhaps, taking the sun on deck and realise
you've lost all sense of what you seek.
Still worse, you haven't checked the lock of hair
you carry round your neck for weeks.

But still you will not turn,
you cover miles. The world
is more enticing than you feared.
You learn to love your sweat,
the manly absence of your tears.

But then suppose one night
you stop in some strange port
and suddenly, there's your man,
but smaller, more stooped; you note
the nervous tremor in his hands.

Suppose he's worse for drink
and telling tales to the assembled crowd.
I remember Ithaka! he cries.
You try to summon tears of joy but nothing comes;
you dare not look him in the eye.

Without him you would never have set out.
He gave you this, the journey,
but is he the destiny you're searching for?
Is he your Ithaka?
Not any more.

You pull the hood over your face.
Head for the door.

Bondage

I once knew a woman who was Houdini's opposite.
No hands, unaided, she had taught herself to gag
her wants with masking tape, shackle her feet,
bind her own wrists in the manner of famous sadists.
She was a smouldering starlet, a five-pointed miracle
artfully arranged on the crispness of linen.
She'd brand the mattress with her hourglass
of flesh while she waited for her man to save her
and sure enough he'd always turn up just in time
ready to rip the tape from her lips, slit the knots,
turn the key and set her free to perform her act
over and over, each time with more of that slick,
irresistible conviction. What pleasure was there.
She called it love. He called it getting a grip.

Six feet of New Linen

Do you remember our first, narrow bed?
It coaxed us close, our breath mixing to mist
that hid our fears and blemishes and fed
the myth of easy love and coupled bliss.

For years, I've mapped your web of veins, I've sparred
and stabbed. I've braved uncharted arteries
that spat blood, lapped your tears like milk, plunged far
into your depths, sought out new strategies.
I'll have you yet, I'll draw you in. Not done,
the endless round of touch and tussle, heart
and mouth trying to speak in unison,
so much to hold, so little truly grasped.
  In this expanse of white, you lie beyond
  my reach, waiting for me to take your hand.

Brother of the Gusset

Use her song to pull the string
make your strumpet strut and sing
teach her how to bite her tongue.

Milk the hind who drinks your gin
ink your face into her skin
promise her but don't say when.

Treat the harlot with finesse
filth her poke and tear her dress
bind her hands and kill her kiss.

Give it everything you've got
squeeze the fruit until it rots
tear the gusset, bust the gut.

Streets to walk and time to bruise
cash to count and gash to use
mark her mouth and keep her close.

You would say it's nature's plan:
spike her heels and see her run.
Catch the snatch to feed the man
lost and lusted, crushed and done.

Note: Brother of the Gusset is 18th Century slang for pimp

When you have a new dress anything's possible

Wear no lingerie.
Don't linger

at the mirror.
Step out. And wait.

A sudden gush of crotchets
liquefies the air.

Waves of magenta silk
lap the street,

crowds ride pink surf,
black lace

nets a few fine fish.
The stars gavotte,

a mad moon loops,
and back on land,

even the wolf rolls over,
bares his chest.

You climb ashore for him.
You curve, stiletto,

strut, unzip. Take off
your dress.

Household Tips for the Obliteration of Green

Winning hue on weeping willow, requisite for lettuce, courgette or indeed summer squash, green is always with us.

However: green may present as toad, snake, lizard, mildew, mould or lichen, creeping algae, pigment of witch.

If permitted to settle on tender parts, green may grow ambitious, permeate the skin, sully the net curtains of the heart.

My remedy: to eradicate taint of you know who: continuum from blush to pillarbox, incandescent only as a last resort.

Or try this: crimson flush, as of ruby, fire or lava. Stain his lips with yours, take him open mouthed, one sanguine, lucid bite.

Bocca della Verità

('Mouth of Truth', from a painting by Lucas Cranach the Elder)

The stone beast can't scare me; I've met worse.
Though Lord knows I'm no Audrey Hepburn
playing virgin on a Roman holiday, innocence
is only relative. I won't lie to the brute and he's the one
who matters. I'll look him in the eye until he pants
then plunge the plump fruit of my hand deep
into his mouth and work it hard until the jam
of his ancient maw starts to hurt and he gives in.
Oh, he won't bite, he'll simply loosen, all agog
and gagging. I'll train him up on taste and lick;
I'll give him suck. As for his teeth, they're long gone,
worn flat after centuries, the grind and crack
of liars' bones, not mine. I'm just an honest strumpet
shackled to a man who aches to see me lose a hand
to prove adultery, who dares to call that feeling love.

Keeping House

So now we know the men,
their tricks of love and artifice,

their clever twists
of kiss and distance.

Yet we remain
their fading addicts

slumped in sad cafes
at tutting time, women

long since mutated
into cringe and wheedle.

We who live in mirrors
of our mothers' houses,

study yellowed recipes,
the ancient art of planting

calibrated kisses wrung
from rose and desperation,

we who rock our gurning burdens
as they leak tears and milk,

wait in twilit hallways
poised to tug the big man's boots

and cleanse him of his kill.
We who sometimes look

towards the light that falls
through open doors

who totter on these lofty shoes
we've worn too long for love,

still long for love;
still stir and melt

towards him
as he calls for more

slow tenderness
of meat and marrow.

Crossing the Border

I lived there once: your country
with its flings and razzmatazz,

its itch of sky, no shelter but the arms
of somebody who might not stay.

I don't remember the moment
I gave up the howl of wilderness,

the dirt and slim pickings, even
those shots of joy, and crossed

the border, but I'm long gone.
I've found a more forgiving edge,

come round to these peopled nights,
a sky that's never black, the urban horn

of plenty. You might say that after
circling for years, I've arrived

at myself. You should come and see
my latest work, take its pulse

under neon. Maybe you miss
the shock of us, our furniture

and badinage, my particular eye.
Now tell me what it's like for you.

Triumph Triple R

Suburbia's a blur; visors lowered, ripple
past the multiplex, Ikea, Leatherland. Cars limp
and whine along the 406, beyond all help.
Not us: full of grace, curving into bends, slick tilt
and balance in the wind, arrive at Epping just on time,
helmets misted, eyeballed, respected, triumph
of mud around our boots. It's a new world; trip
and giggle in the line for bacon rolls, salty lure
for all those big-bollocked dogs. High on the rite
of *You be biker I'll be biker chick*, plump
with daring, stripped of restraint, can it hurt
to whoop on take-off, throttle wide, to rule
the road, burn rubber, feel the tarmac melt?

Last Harvest

So when you said asparagus
I took myself to market,
bought the finest I could find.

I scoured my books for recipes:
Apicius, Mrs Beaton,
Elizabeth David, Raymond Blanc.

I prepared asparagus
for every meal: with foaming
hollandaise, vinaigrette,

green and white with truffles
and without,
oven-roasted in olive oil,

airy in soufflés, liquidised
for soup. I watched for signs
from you as I fed you tips

from a silver spoon: nothing.
You chewed and swallowed
but still you didn't give me

The Look. So I got down
on my knees, staked out
the garden in perfect rows,

raised more asparagus
from seed. I dug
my own furrows, tended

thinned and weeded till my skin
was the colour of earth.
While you slept, I kept watch

for thieves and creeping things,
and when the plants were ripe,
I fed them all to you.

But soon my crop was gone,
my garden barren;
I laced my boots

and commandeered
allotments to grow more.
I watered my asparagus,

talked to them, stroked
their stems, sprayed
their feathered leaves.

While you languished
fat and hungry in the sun,
I told them my love,

and they grew tall as totems,
beautiful, but you consumed
them all. So I bulldozed

ancient woodlands, cleared
more acres, annexed farms,
killed crops. Cows

had nowhere left to graze.
Wildflowers died.
Still your hunger gnawed at me.

I razed the towns and left
the dispossessed camped out
between rows of asparagus

but still you would not change
even as I stuffed you with my harvest
till your face turned slowly green.

It was then I bound you –
neck and wrist with strings of berries,
dressed your mouth with yellow petals.

Though you did not speak again
you were alert and growthful
as you ate the light.

Your limbs lengthened,
your feet grew roots.
I took up my spade and dug

a wide furrow; and there
below my window, the earth
newly turned, I planted you.

After a Long Sleep

she woke and said

My dreams were oceans
earth and curve
the dizzy tilt and spill of you and I
the rise and fall of many moons
a sweet hot sigh.

I don't remember mine
he answered
reaching for his tie.

Lost Property

Since we parted I have lost my red wrap. This is a symptom.
I grow pale, I want my roses, I want to be fed, I make it difficult.
You will find my red wrap on the other woman, the one who sees
only what's in front of her, who took it from a sofa where I left it.
Crimson is not her colour but now she basks in my heat and wears
the smell of my longing on her shoulders. Salted with flakes
of my skin and yours, she is all smiles, she is always replete.
If she had the eye she would touch my mind, she would read
my scrawls, she would balk at my famished words, circling.
But she doesn't have the eye. I have the eye and I have the greed
and she has my red wrap and she has caught you inside it.
Oh, but sweetheart, how easy she makes it for you, she who has
such appetites. I do not see you struggle as she tightens the knot.

The Goods

Sweetheart, these are not
the gifts you asked for
but allow me to present
this clever machine
of my own flesh
which measures distance
by the unit of ache.

I am giving you
the pointless telephone
the dark you left me
to stumble through
and these two knees
blooded from tripping up
on all our mistakes.

You may take this pile of ash
from the touch papers
that never caught
the scree of your words
the waste, the overflow
the blocks of silence
you try to pretend are mine

but I am not ready to hand over
the wilful stain of your lips
or this gasp I keep for you
in the nest of my throat
or the praise-tongue
that still hangs by a thread
from the bell of my mouth.

Geometry

Remember how, one night not long ago
you told our daughter what you'd read
about infinity? I couldn't understand,
although you drew a diagram
to show that two parallel lines,
if left to run forever, will eventually meet.
Remember when she came home
crying the next day covered in shame.
In front of everyone her teacher
had dismissed her father's proof.
But I believe you. If you and I had never met
that rainy night in Camden Town,
if that night had never been,
that's where we'd be, each walking the line
towards infinity, searching for the place
where the impossible can happen
and two parallel lines collide.

III

*'Shortly shall all my labours end and thou
Shalt have the air at freedom'*

William Shakespeare

To My Daughter, Naked

I ache to go back
to your country

where once I lived
where there is no eye

of the mirror, no lens,
no spectator.

I ache to forget
these breasts

to spread my legs
without meaning.

I Thought I Saw my Mother on the BBC,

orchid behind
one ear, queen
of the Groucho

toned legs casual
in those hotpants
that I coveted for years.

She was *like this*
with Zadie Smith
and Melvyn Bragg.

Of course she'd wed
again: Arthur Miller,
or was it Johnny Depp,

she glowed with Pulitzer,
daily hot sex, a diet
of yellow-fin tuna.

I thought I saw my mother
on the BBC,
Nobel Laureate.

Sinuous in off-the-shoulder
Vera Wang and collagen,
she leaned

into the lectern,
articulated low towards
the microphone.

You should have seen
my mother's breasts,
their rise and globe,

and she so eloquent
on Dante, Cerberus,
Schroedinger's cat.

Truth be told
I often think
I see my mother, but

it's just another
murky tryst
in some imagined heaven

where she's still high
and tight in those hotpants
that passed to me

too late, stretched
to hell and back,
long out of fashion.

Seventeen and all that Shit

You wore *ugly* like seventies corridors wore their skin
of anaglypta. Your ugly wink flickered like the *vacant* signs

that beckoned from motorways; twitched in dayglo mirrors
in hotel lifts. You fastened *ugly* round your neck in strands

like fake pearls, took it naked to bed with third rate
touring drummers, taxi drivers, men with diaries and wives;

you flaunted *ugly* like cheap knickers retrieved on many
pinked-up mornings, sun rising like a boil. You let your *ugly*

seep into these envelopes of photographs carried home
from chemists, and you turned your head away.

But now you stare, blinded, at these clean sheets
of negatives, backlit with hindsight. There was no *ugly*;

only youth with its tilted longings, and those myths
written in lipstick on the mirror, the ones you took for truth.

In the Morning She Wears Red

The ancient freezer
drops ice in the night.

Duet of sob and cry,
of grunt and gasp, leaks

through the wall.
My thin dreams are glass

broken on concrete
but mother glitters

in the morning.
Sex is like oxygen, she says,

pouring the coffee,
there's no virtue

in virginity. Don't eat that.
You have your father's legs.

Meal after meal for weeks
the hard-boiled egg

relinquishes its shell
but sulphurs the mouth,

the grapefruit fights
the spoon, the inches cling.

I hunt my skeleton
in the high circle of mirror:

I want her to applaud
my clavicle, my ribs,

I want to turn myself
inside out, to bury

this new flesh inside
a carapace of bone.

Triptych

Mother

Four times I was in that place. I leaned so far
into the hot centre of the wind, plunged belly-first
down into the dark birthing water
where howling creatures
push and clamour and cling.

Four times I was in that place, four times
torn, four times delivered
from my drowning.
That part was simple.
It was all that followed
that left me gasping for breath.

Madonna

Dig for the dark oriels of eyes, the bone-deep
ache in the shoulders, the animal openness concealed
by conjurers beneath layers of faded pigment.

She cannot move. There, pinned against the wall,
she must remain forever feeding, bleeding
her secrets into the landfills of history.

Never trust those fast and artful men who hid
the spread of red in wet plaster behind
the false colours of a thousand frescoes.

Passing by the Playground at Highgate Wood

They're like bedraggled birds
gone to fat, these unsexed creatures,
blurred at the edges,
pushing swings and burbling
nonsense words in Mother-tongue.

I'm not stopping.
Not for long.
Just watching the ghost of me,
chest marked by two dark circles
like targets
leaking love
into the world's mouth.

Lambskin

Spring child, you turned up late
and restless, for weeks you wouldn't sleep
without a nipple in your mouth.

Stupidly, I thought there could be nothing worse,
prop-eyed for nights on end, tethered to you,
wakened hourly, at the edge of madness.

The lambskin rescued both of us.
Your cries would muffle, comfort in its fluff,
the scent of talcum, sweat and baby-sick,

the simplified, miraculous outline
of a small animal at rest, replete
with mother's milk, too new for grass,

a safe lining for your speechless dreams.
This was your first turn away, my first longed-for
hint of freedom from the tug and suck.

I thought of it last March, *lambskin*,
when we drove across the Severn Bridge
past green pastures, your long limbs cramping

in the back, the crunch of crisps, the crackled
beat of ipod. I reached behind to bother you,
touched your warm cheek, just checking,

on the way to the wake. No hurry now to let you go.
There was the boy who shared your birthday,
ashes scattered to the wind; his mother, father,

knowing truly what the worst can be, knee-deep
in sodden earth, distant in rising mist.
There were lambs in the next field, brazen

in the innocence of nudge and suckle,
their stupid-eyed, impatient mothers
feeding at the very edge of spring.

Retainer

You left a scattering of dark mascara,
scent of artificial tropics, no room
for negotiation, front door, oddly, still ajar.
I remembered too late, called, but you
were i-tuned out of it. Your plastic palate
with its list of Do's and Don'ts rattled on
inside my bag, a disembodied replicate
moulded to force a smile. And you were gone.

It all comes back now; I can feel the marvel
of your mouth at work with its voracious tongue,
hot mix of blood and milk, the flinch and thrill.
Here we go again: the let-down, nothing new:
thin, bluish leak of memory, a gush of cradle song
the shade of gin perhaps, or sap, or glue.

After Love

I didn't like my mother's boyfriends much.
In fact she wasn't keen on them herself
but feared the worst: ending up on the shelf.
How terrible, she said, to stay untouched,
unheld, while slowly growing old. She judged
it wise, (abandoned for a newer, sylph-
like model wife), to guard her mental health
by *taking lovers*, like pills; unattached,
unburdened, selfish men, who'd help her find
salvation in a hardened heart. Of course
there'd be no pain. Just sex, a second youth.
I met these men sometimes. They weren't unkind.
We'd nod, then part like co-conspirators
in some veiled plot to save her from the truth.

Driving Licence

This isn't mine to withhold or to give:
your paper pass to danger. I long to reel
you in and tie you down, I want to cling
to you like peach to stone. Honey, stay. I'd even
bribe you with a chauffeured, meals-included ride
to Kathmandu to keep you, but you just want to drive.
Okay, you've gone from shudder, clutch and grind
to smooth - you're still a novice on the white-line
risks and chances of the road. But how can I grieve
to see you at the wheel, tossing me that big-man grin,
eyes wide open, ready for it? Go on. Take off. Live.

Forgotten

It's the name of your doctor, the measure of sugar,
a world famous author; the Spanish for butter,
that African river, the age of your child
or your lover. No cure.

It leaks, a lexicon dripper, a seep from your ears
while you sleep. Flotillas of skiffs with their cargo
of words set off in the dark, no hand at the tiller,
sail into the yonder.

A sheet of blank sea lies beneath a white aura.
The further you look, the wider and stiller your ocean.
The storms and the fever, the waver and flounder
are sure to come later.

You'll never recapture those words going under.
All you can do is jabber and shiver. The witter
of lingo abandoned forever, the steady procession
of drifter and sinker,

of rotter and drowner. Those depths are like murder.
Your words are the bones of the dead
decomposing in water.

On the Road

Today you find you're crying at old photographs
like your mother did: the slim trunk of that willow
propped against a bamboo stick in the wind,
your downy babies moulded to their father's side,
the boy you loved who died under a speeding car.
Suddenly you drive just like your fledgling daughter
with her L plates, wary of potholes, speed bumps,
boys who lie in wait to dart in front of you and bend
tomorrow out of joint. Those yesterdays you shelved away
nudge at you like that boy in his souped-up cabriolet
who hovers inches from your bumper till you let him pass,
watch him speed towards a future he can't yet countenance:
blind curves, lost decades, and if luck is on his side,
an album full of photographs to make him cry.

Last Call

After months of hide and seek, of truth and dare,
the pills, the ills, the physio, the *don't despair*
those broken cells beyond repair,
you dialled me again, but I wasn't there
and so you called up Death and told her
where you were. Seconds later
she was slumped down in your favourite chair,
weeping as if this longed-for coda
might be something you could share.
Walk with me, Death, you said, *let's end this sad affair.*
So Death, who'd had forever to prepare,
said *Yes my Darling*. And off you wandered,
arm in arm, a perfect pair.
She guided you to the appointed place,
stretched out one dainty foot
and tripped you up on the concrete stair.
After the crack, your brain unanchored
in your skull, that blinding resonance
with Death was more than you could bear.
Love me, Death, you begged, *show me you care.*
Death sat a while and watched you
gasp and snatch at the un-giving air
before she flicked her switchblade,
scalped you then and there.
The last you knew, you heard her swear
she loved you more than I: who knows?
Perhaps that's fair enough: it was Death,
not I, who said a prayer,
who dropped the final silence in your ear,
your dark head cradled in her lap, not mine,
her bloodied fingers in your hair.

Cutting the Pear

I wonder if there are pears where you are now,
whether we might share one again.

I never liked the way you sliced towards
your hand, green globe cradled in your palm;

there might be blood surely
and you'd been wounded enough already.

You make the first incision;
blunt knife, resistant flesh.

Two separated halves now lie face to face
with pips for eyes. I want to say I'm sorry

but I don't. That would be too easy now.
Instead, I let the scene run on.

You core and peel the pear,
offer me the first slice. I take it.

Assumption

You were always on the prowl: you'd find
some lofty, careless window, fix your sights
on him below. You never landed on your feet.
Not like our cat who once gave chase, escaped
through the narrow kitchen sash and dropped
a hundred metres, enchanted by the mate
she never caught. After all the flying fur
and panic, the vet we never could afford,
it seems unjust. Our mad cat lived to lust
and leap another day, but you, you'd fall
and fracture every time, until you landed
on your head, my tiny mother. Not much
the clever man with thread and clamps
could do with clots like that, so up you shot
into the blue. You ditched your grubby wings
and swore on the ascent as if you were
some crazed madonna, spitting fire,
halo on the tilt, still longing for her Lucifer.

Thank you for buying *The Kitchen of Lovely Contraptions*. While it is Jacqueline Saphra's first full collection, she has published other work prior to this.

You can find more information on the author at:
http://www.jacqueline.saphra.net

—§—

the waterways series is an imprint of flipped eye publishing, a small publisher dedicated to publishing powerful new voices in affordable volumes. Founded in 2001, we have won awards and international recognition through our focus on publishing fiction and poetry that is clear and true, rather than exhibitionist.

If you would like more information about flipped eye publishing, please join our mailing list online at **www.flippedeye.net**.

Lightning Source UK Ltd.
Milton Keynes UK
175738UK00003B/3/P